Direct 'n Succeed

MISTAKES COMPANIES MAKE WITH
RECRUITING AND RETENTION
AND
HOW TO AVOID THEM

Julie Still-Rolin
Professional Development Specialist

An organization's ability to learn, and translate that learning into action rapidly, is the ultimate competitive advantage.
— *Jack Welch, Former CEO of General Electric*

Direct 'n Succeed Copyright © 2018 by Julie Still-Rolin. All Rights Reserved.

All rights reserved. No part of this book may be reproduced in any form or by any electronic or mechanical means including information storage and retrieval systems, without permission in writing from the author. The only exception is by a reviewer, who may quote short excerpts in a review.

Names, characters, places, and incidents either are products of the author's imagination or are used fictitiously. Any resemblance to actual persons, living or dead, events, or locales is entirely coincidental.

Julie Still-Rolin
Visit my website at www.juliestillrolin.com

Printed in the United States of America

First Printing: Nov 2018

ISBN- 9781081429317

Dedicated to my wife, who made this book possible with all of her daily rants.

CONTENTS

Introduction 6

Mistake #1: 8

Mistake #2: 15

Mistake #3: 24

Mistake #4: 30

Mistake #5: 38

Chapter 6: Review Workbook 46

Introduction

AS A PROFESSIONAL DEVELOPMENT SPECIALIST, my job is to observe the problems that companies face and create solutions to those problems. The problems addressed in this book were born out of these observations related to recruiting and retaining the best and brightest employees. The solutions were derived from research and experience. This book provides an examination of the problems with recruiting and retention, easy-to-implement solutions, and a handy workbook (Chapter 6) in hopes of helping companies direct and succeed.

To be competitive and successful, companies must be willing to evaluate their processes and procedures and make the changes necessary when needed. When dealing with people, this is especially true. Many companies have recognized the need to amp up their game in recruiting and retaining the best and the brightest employees.

In 2018, having a college degree is equivalent to having a high school diploma. This qualification no longer sets a person apart. With the growth in access to public education, the value of degrees alone is decreasing. Instead, employers should be paying more attention to the unique strengths of candidates and employees that go beyond the skills obtained in school. For instance, a person may have a degree in business but have no experience in sales. The degree does not translate into the personal relationship building skills that are necessary for sales. Being able to identify and recognize strengths beyond minimum qualifications is a major step in improving job placement.

Job placement issues also continue as time progresses. The adage, "Familiarity breeds contempt" can be applied here. People get burned out. Monotonous activities can lead to boredom and a sense of uselessness. Leaders need to recognize this and, instead of accepting the old way of doing things, make efforts to create a better workplace environment.

The environment should also be safe and free from negativity. Everyone needs to work. Otherwise, we'd all be sitting on a beach somewhere drinking Pina Coladas. And, everyone has put in some form of effort to obtain his or her position. This effort may look different for different people, but this is not what is important. What is important is that people should not be subjected to hostile work environments, and companies must take proactive measures to prevent these instead of sweeping problems under the rug or chopping them off as normal.

Your company should strive for its "normal" to be a safe, fun, challenging, and fulfilling place to work. This will add to your corporate social responsibility. And, most importantly, it will help you recruit and retain the best and brightest employees. This can only be accomplished by actively directing the company towards success.

Mistake #1:
Swing 'n Miss
STRIKING OUT ON THE FIRST IMPRESSION

BASEBALL PLAYERS BECOME KNOWN FOR THEIR BATTING STATS. If you strike out the first time you're up to bat, people are going to expect you to strike out every time. Studies have proven that other people's perceptions of you can lead to the way that they treat you, which leads to the way that you treat yourself. Zig Ziglar tells a story in one of his talks about how he became the best salesman after his idol showed confidence in him. In business, as in all areas of life, for every action, there is an equal and opposite reaction. This is scientific; this is law. And, this applies to the impression that your business makes on others as well: For every action that your business takes, there is an equal 'n opposite reaction.

Jody began looking for a new position within the first year she was promoted as manager. She was finally in a position where she had a BATNA (Better Alternative to a Negotiated Agreement) (Fisher, Ury, & Patton, 2011). This is important for business leaders to understand because the best and brightest employees position themselves so that they have an alternative that is at least equal to if not better than the position they are applying for.

What does this mean for you? You should be focusing on positioning your company as the BATNA.

Jody had taken the time to develop her skills as a manager and hospitality specialist. She developed and implemented processes that improve procedures and developed systems for managing employees well. She earned her degree in business administration and has several years of experience. Also, she has a great personality and strives to be the best at what she does. Overall, she has a lot to offer. She is the best and the brightest candidate for many positions.

She also determined her values: flexibility, financial success, respect, recognition, and fun (probably not in that order).

When the best and the brightest apply for a position, they have more than likely followed these steps as well.

When Jody is searching for her new position, she is looking for companies that share her values. These companies are the ones who get selected by the best and the brightest.

If your company is missing the ball on the first impression by not having and demonstrating strong values, you are missing out on attracting the best candidates. YOUR COMPANY SHOULD BECOME THE BATNA.

♦♦♦ Why Is It Important to BECOME THE BATNA? ♦♦♦

You will protect your company from being forced to choose a candidate that is not the best and the brightest.

You will be able to make the most of what you have to offer in order to generate a strong mutual relationship with the best candidate.

You will attract the best and the brightest candidates.

The BATNA concept was developed for negotiation preparation. It gives the negotiator power and leverage. If you apply this concept to seeking the best and brightest candidates for your company, you can see that you want to offer the best situation so that you can in turn receive the best candidate.

How To Become The BATNA

If you'd like to position your company as the best alternative to a negotiated agreement for the best and brightest candidates, you should apply these steps:

1. Establish or Revisit Your Vision Statement and Make Sure It Exhibits Strong Values.

2. Demonstrate How These Values Are Accomplished Through Actions Taken By The Company.

3. Continuously Evaluate, Assess, and Improve.

As Jody looks at companies that she may want to join, she searches for those companies that exhibit the values that she has established for herself personally and professionally. In this competitive market, we cannot dismiss people's interests. After all, interests are what drive people. If their interests are not obtained, they will be driven to seek other opportunities. If their interests are obtained, they will be more productive and loyal.

Recall that Jody's values were flexibility, financial success, respect, recognition, and fun. Let's assume that these are pretty common and look at some ways to apply the concepts of becoming the BATNA.

Vision: To be the best _____company and offer the best _____services while developing an excellent environment for our tribe through flexible work schedules, competitive pay, emphasis on individuality and appreciation, and most importantly, having fun.

Notice that this is generic and may not be your vision, but what is important here is that it displays some values that align with Jody's.

Now, that sounds good, but words are nothing without action behind them. So, how can your company demonstrate those values?

Look at some of the model companies that successfully demonstrate their values:

One of my favorites is Publix:

Our mission at Publix is to be the premier quality food retailer in the world.
To that end, we commit to be:
- *Passionately focused on customer value,*
- *Intolerant of waste,*
- *Dedicated to the dignity, value and employment security of our associates,*
- *Devoted to the highest standards of stewardship for our stockholders, and*
- *Involved as responsible citizens in our communities.*
Retrieved from:
http://corporate.publix.com/about-publix/company-overview/mission-statement-guarantee

Publix's Mission Statement demonstrates the company's values, which highlight the founder's altruistic vision.

To take this further, the company's website is set up to demonstrate how these values are accomplished. One means of doing this is through the company's commitment to giving:

> *Our Spirit of Giving*
> Once asked what he would be worth today if he hadn't given so much away, Publix founder George Jenkins immediately responded, "Probably nothing." And his legacy of giving continues today.
>
> Publix and Publix Charities give to local food banks and other nonprofits each year, and some donations are made with the generous help of our customers and associates.
>
> Publix and Publix Charities also support a variety of nonprofits that help youth in our communities, including Camp Boggy Creek, Big Brothers Big Sisters, Scout programs, and many others. Associates and customers can contribute to help local youth through donation programs such as Tools for Back to School.
> Retrieved from:
> http://corporate.publix.com/community/corporate-campaigns

When companies fail to recognize these very important factors of business, they put themselves at higher risk for turnover and other costly consequences. Currently, and with younger generations of talented workers entering the workforce, companies must find new ways to recruit and retain good employees. This starts with being the best alternative to a negotiated agreement. In this case, the agreement is hiring the best and brightest, and to be the BATNA here, the company must establish their values and follow through with demonstrating them.

You may be an excellent batter. Your stats may be fantastic, but if you do not continuously improve, a new player may come along and shine brighter or hit harder. When it comes to business, improvement is the difference between a swing 'n a hit or a swing 'n a miss.

Mistake #2:

Shake 'n Bake

NOT HIRING THE BEST FIT AND/OR KEEPING THEM IN THE WRONG POSITION

Shake 'n Bake boasts that it is so easy, a child can do it: "It's Shake 'n Bake, and I helped," keeps getting stuck in my head as I write this chapter. Unfortunately, most business processes take skill beyond a six-year-old who wants to help in the kitchen. They also require more than just skills. In his book, *Think and Grow Rich,* Napoleon Hill discusses how anyone can acquire an education, and this does not always equal knowledge. The same concept applies to specific positions at specific companies. Just because someone meets the requirements does not always mean that that person is the best fit. Hiring the wrong person for a position is a common mistake, but it can be remedied.

This chapter will present three ways of overcoming "Shake 'n Bake" syndrome (or assuming that *anyone* can do it). First of all, we will look at creating a job posting that allows the employer to not only understand the requirements, but also forces the employer to examine the personality and qualities that will be necessary for the position. Then we'll look at team building. In this context, team building is not traditional. Instead, team building is presented as a way for companies to evaluate new hires after they have an opportunity to demonstrate their strengths and weaknesses, and then place them in a more permanent position. Finally, we'll examine the concept of job rotation, which allows the company to make changes based on organizational needs and avoid keeping the wrong person in the wrong position.

♦♦♦ New Job Postings ♦♦♦

The traditional job posting needs to be revisited, especially if a company is experiencing high turnover rates as this indicates that some percentage of employees were not hired correctly, which is most likely due to a miscommunication in the job posting. In order to avoid this problem, companies should follow a simple model that covers the needs of the organization while also displaying their personality. This will help potential candidates make better informed decisions when seeking a position.

Job Descriptions Should:

1. *Be short yet concise*
2. *Demonstrate the absolute requirements of the job (the necessities not the preferred qualities)*
3. *Share some of the company's personality*

When constructing a job description, you should also consider flexibility on the absolutes. Of course, if the position is for an IT Security Manager, you will not be able to justify flexibility in the requirements of IT security skills, BUT, many people these days have taught themselves more than a program can teach them. DO NOT TAKE THE VALUABLE ASSETS OFF THE TABLE FOR YOUR COMPANY JUST TO FILL A TECHNICAL REQUIREMENT.

For instance, I have a master's degree in English, but my skills are not limited to writing and research (contrary to most job postings requiring my degree). In fact, I have successfully managed two businesses, and I am great at coordinating events. None of these ventures really have anything to do with my degree other than it demonstrates my excellent communication skills and perseverance. I'm not bragging about my abilities, but I am trying to make a point. I got a degree in English because I thought that that was what I was good at and what I loved. I had no idea what I was really good at when I was in my twenties. In fact, I would go as far as to say that my degree was more personal development than a path to a profession. Does this limit me from getting a position at a company where I could be a valuable asset as an event coordinator or in some other position? If the employer is not flexible on the absolute requirements, yes.

The key to attracting the best and the brightest candidates is to be clear in the job description and to be open to possibilities outside of the restricted requirements. Being clear includes you and the candidate having clarity. If you know exactly what you need, you also know exactly what you can and cannot budge on. Being open includes recognizing that technical requirements do not always lead to the best fit.

♦♦♦ Team Building Candidates ♦♦♦

In the past, Team Building was reserved for putting together a group with already assigned duties, and this is a great model. Why not use teams as a trial to determine proper placement as well?

Team building candidacy projects marry the concepts of team building and trial period. They allow employers to evaluate candidates based on their abilities rather than how they present themselves in an interview. They also give candidates the opportunity to determine if they truly want to work with the team.

Should you attempt a team building candidacy project? You should consider it if you can meet the following factors:

1. *Your company allows flexibility in developing positions.*
2. *Your company understands the need to improve hiring processes.* *
3. *Your company has the resources to sustain a trial team building candidacy project. (This will vary based on the needs of the company).*

*In developing this theory, I reached out to managers and hiring supervisors. They agreed that their current hiring process (posting a job, interviewing, and hiring a candidate) was not sufficient, and they often ended up with high turnover rates and/or costly factors such as low productivity due to stress and dissatisfaction.

How To Develop and Implement a Team Building Candidacy Program

If you're interested in improving the hiring process to recruit and retain the best and the brightest employees, follow these steps:

1. Develop a plan: Establish the needs, create a process for meeting the needs, and include all necessary details, such as expected outcomes.
2. Establish a time-frame and budget for the project and get approval if needed.
3. Launch the project: Publish job posting with details on project contingency and trial basis.
4. Continuously Evaluate, Assess, and Improve the Program by documenting best and worst practices thoroughly.

This research into a new way to improve the hiring process was prompted by years of observation. More people than I can count have expressed discontentment with their jobs because they were placed in a position that did not help them reach their potential. This dissatisfaction leads to lower productivity, stress, and eventually the desire to search for another position. Placing the wrong person in a management position can lead to these effects on all of the people being managed by the wrong person. ALL OF THE PEOPLE BEING MANAGED BY THE WRONG PERSON WILL BE LESS PRODUCTIVE, HIGHLY STRESSED, AND EXTREMELY UNHAPPY.

Frank is a good example of this. Frank was hired as a manager of a call center for a group of hotels. He had never worked in a call center before, but the job posting called for a bachelor's degree in business and managerial experience, which he possessed. Frank never took the time to learn the processes of the call center. He relied heavily on the supervisors to handle problems with the processes. Instead of properly managing his teams, he avoided the office as much as possible. He planned employee events, and he spent most of his time driving between centers and attending meetings that he knew nothing about. The result of Frank's management was chaos. Employees did not respect him, so they were not productive. They manipulated him because he did not understand all the policies and procedures. The supervisors and others were overwhelmed with work, and they were unhappy because of the lack of support they received from Frank.

Frank would have been better positioned as an event coordinator. He did a really good job of putting together employee outings, team building exercises, and holiday parties. However, he was not manager material.

Had Frank been given a project as part of the hiring process, this would have been obvious. However, the project would have needed to be aligned with his MANAGERIAL duties. For instance, he would have needed to be presented with a project that involved MANAGERIAL skills. THIS IS VITAL TO THE SUCCESS OF THE TEAM BUILDING CANDIDACY PROJECT. When you're developing the project, make sure that the project assigns duties that are specific to the expected responsibilities of the position. Of course, the candidate should not be expected to know the processes and procedures of the company, so you'll need to choose a project that requires the least knowledge of specifics necessary but still highlights the abilities required.

♦ ♦ ♦ Job Rotation ♦ ♦ ♦

Sometimes we get so caught up in trying to do things the "right" way that we forget creativity. As cultures evolve, so should businesses. In this new "Gig" economy, people have changed the way that work is accomplished, and businesses who want to recruit and retain the best and the brightest must do some changing too. However, this does not always mean cleaning house and starting over. Instead, it could mean a simple job rotation.

Job rotation is defined as the systematic movement of workers from job to job to improve job satisfaction, reduce boredom, and enable employees to gain a broad perspective over the work process within the entire organization (Walker, 2013).

Perhaps your company does not have the resources to implement a team building candidacy program or is simply not looking to hire new employees but rather utilize the current talent better. Job rotation would be the solution.

In many professions, higher positions require experience in lower positions so that people can learn the processes and procedures to better manage them and be empathetic with others in those positions. For instance, principals must have teaching experience prior to becoming a principal. This is valid reasoning that should be applied to all professions. However, job rotation also offers parallel employees to switch roles and better understand every facet of the organization. While this may not be feasible for every position at every company, it should be considered.

Let's apply job rotation to Frank. If after several months of employment as the manager, it is recognized that Frank is not effectively managing the call center, he should be considered for job rotation. How would this work? Frank would be placed in a new position that is necessary and reflects his abilities.

To fairly replace Frank, candidates for manager would be chosen from the supervisors on the team. As you can see, this takes a lot of effort and decision making. However, it is not impossible. Of course, Frank would not be demoted, so he would still carry some of his responsibilities. This would justify him keeping his current salary, and it would satisfy the new manager's need for a manageable workload. Let's call Frank's new position "Event Coordinator and Team Morale Builder." This position suits him much better, and it takes the responsibility of these tasks off the new manager.

Some of you are probably wondering who will replace the supervisor who moves into the manager position. Good question. In this case, no one. Instead of hiring someone new or promoting someone, the call center will simply reevaluate and reassign teams to the current supervisors. With new management being a better fit, the supervisors will be more productive and happier. As with any new program, this will be customized based on the organization, assessed and evaluated, and the best practices will be recorded for future reference.

Shake 'n Bake is a great product, but the concept should not be applied to hiring procedures. Great companies recognize the need to try new methods. It does not mean that whoever came up with the old methods was wrong; it simply means that it's time for a new blend of herbs 'n spices. It is time to recognize the strengths that employees have and place them in positions that align with those strengths.

Mistake #3:

Hit 'n Run

HIRING THE BEST, BUT NOT USING THEIR TALENTS

MISTAKES HAPPEN. THIS IS INEVITABLE. HOWEVER, HOW WE CHOOSE TO RESPOND TO MISTAKES is more important than the mistake itself. People who mistakenly cause an accident are not held at fault as long as they are not responsible. However, people who mistakenly cause an accident and run rather than facing their mistake and helping are held at fault for their response to their mistake. When discussing the habits of effective people, Stephen Covey writes that the power to choose how to respond is what makes us human. When it comes to recruiting and retention, hiring is only half the battle. Mistakenly misusing team members' talents can be detrimental in many ways, but leaders have the opportunity to respond properly to this mistake and recover.

To avoid "Hit 'n Run," employers should be prepared to face the possibility of mistakenly misusing talent. This requires evaluation, planning, and recognition.

This chapter was also inspired by Jody's experience. Jody began working in call centers by chance. A friend of hers told her of an opportunity, so she went for it. Although being a call center agent was not necessarily Jody's career plan, she is the type of person to take initiative and be great. She quickly moved from agent to supervisor. In this role, she went above and beyond. She created processes that improved systems, and she developed her own impressive time management and organizational methods. She found fulfillment in making things better.

When her manager informed her that she would be leaving, Jody volunteered to learn as much as she could about managing guest services. Of all the supervisors, she was the only one who took this initiative. She made herself invaluable. Her director came to her and informed her that he had taken notice and that she would be taking over the call center. However, when it was time for the transition, Frank was chosen over her. She was then required to basically train Frank who had never learned the processes and procedures to do the job that she had been preparing for. Frank was incompetent in many ways. One of these was in sexual harassment. He made inappropriate comments, showed favoritism, and was accused of inappropriate acts. Jody was only a witness to many of his inappropriate behaviors, but a seed of discontent had been planted in her. She felt helpless.

Eventually, the work environment became so chaotic for Jody that she could no longer maintain her position as the lead supervisor. She was transferred to another position with less responsibility and more money so that she would not leave the company.

Finally, after Frank had basically run out of options, he was transferred to another center's manager position, and Jody was put in her rightful place. However, it was too late. After being in this position for only a few months, she decided that she had outgrown the company and began seeking other opportunities.

♦ ♦ ♦ P o i s o n   C o n t r o l ♦ ♦ ♦

The above scenario is how people and companies get poisoned. It only takes one experience or one bad person to create chaos, hostility, and discontent. These factors lead to negative responses from employees.

Poisons	*Common Responses*
Not Being Recognized	Seeking Other Opportunities
Undue Favoritism	Helplessness
Being Overlooked	Stealing Company Time
Hostile Work Environment	Stress/Sickness
Overlooking Negative Behavior	Sabotage
Sexual Harassment	Low/No Productivity

All of the above responses cost companies tremendously. NEGATIVE BEHAVIORS AND TREATMENT OF VALUABLE EMPLOYEES CAN DAMAGE THE BOTTOM LINE.

If you think that there may be poison seeping through the veins of your company, you're probably right. Ask yourself these questions to confirm this possibility:

1. *Is there an employee that excels in his/her current role but may be suited for a higher position?*
2. *How do you recognize excellency in your company?*
3. *Is there someone who may be in a position that he/she is not really suited for?*
4. *Is there a lack of productivity?*
5. *Are people taking a lot of time off?**

*High rates of absence may indicate discontent.

How To Exercise Poison Control

If you suspect that there may be some of these issues in your company, there are steps that you can take to remedy this problem:

1. Determine that you will face the problem head on.
2. Evaluate the current climate by surveying employees.*
3. Investigate survey responses.
4. Take action.**

*The surveys should be customized for the organization, so the questions will be determined by the project leader and aimed at discovering the specific issues faced by employees.

**For instance, if the surveys reveal that employees feel that a manager shows favoritism to a certain employee, address this with the manager.

Unfortunately, there are times when nothing can be done. In Jody's situation, this was the case. It did not matter how many times she was given a raise or moved, the environment had become one that she could no longer thrive within. The key is to be as proactive as possible.

Determine from the beginning or now that your company will recognize excellence and hard work. Determine what that looks like. Also determine that your company will not tolerate inappropriate behavior. This will be addressed thoroughly in the next chapter.

♦♦♦ Vision Alignment ♦♦♦

I recently met with a local business owner, and she said something that stood out to me. She said, "I've had people thank me for firing them." At first, I was like, "Yeah, right, no one *wants* to be fired." But, she explained that she recognized that they were not happy. She also recognized that this lack of happiness and fulfillment was not good for her business no matter how much it might cost her. So, she would go to them and say, "I know that you are not happy here, and I want to let you go." They would see the benefit of these words and be grateful. She was able to recognize that their visions did not align.

A key role for leaders is to create a vision for others of what is possible for the organization to achieve (Dyer, et al., 2013). They should also be able to recognize when visions do not align and make the proper adjustments.

When Jody finally decided to go to her director to discuss her discontent instead of just leaving him in the dark, he was understanding. He actually offered to help her in her new search for an alternative opportunity. He recognized that she is talented and that just because her vision no longer aligns with this company's that she will be valuable elsewhere.

He also asked her for feedback. This is true leadership. Her leaving somewhat indicates that he failed her in some way, but instead of being angry, he wants to learn and grow from these mistakes.

Ideally, no one would ever commit a hit 'n run. Everyone everywhere would face their mistakes head on. They would want to take care of the ones that they affect. They would want to grow by learning from their mistakes. Whether you have a new business or one that is well-established does not matter. If you want to evolve and thrive, you must take action and make efforts to recognize your employees' talents and utilize them to their fullest potential.

Mistake #4:
Hide 'n Not Seek

LOSING THE GAME BY NOT BUILDING THE RIGHT CULTURE

NO ONE EVER WANTS TO BE "IT" IN HIDE 'N SEEK, BUT WITHOUT AN "IT," EVERYONE WOULD JUST BE HIDING. Unfortunately, this is the approach that companies take on complex issues. Rather than seeking, they all hide. The issues that I'm talking about are sexual harassment and diversity. Many companies want #MeToo to go away. They want to continue buying doughnuts and popping on an online training session in hopes that the movement will just be a moment and pass on. NEWSFLASH: This is not happening. It's time to start seeking, which means be proactive and make change.

As the Sexual Harassment Guru, I could go on and on about how important it is for companies to improve their culture and create an environment that is not conducive to sexual harassment. I could spout out statistics for days. However, I'm sure everyone has read, seen and heard these over and over. The truth is simple: sexual harassment is bad for business. Period. The other truth is that preventing sexual harassment is good for business. It raises the bottom line. Fortunately, I have created SIMPLE solutions for companies to avoid sexual harassment, sexual harassment liability, and sexual harassment litigation.

The key is to get away from the old way of doing things in which avoidance and/or check the box compliance was the answer.

♦♦♦ The Problem ♦♦♦

When it comes to sexual harassment, the act itself is not *the problem*. Yep, that was not a typo. Compare sexual harassment to theft. When a company sells goods, it knows that theft is inevitable. Theft is not *the problem*. The problem that can be solved is whether or not the company has the correct level of security. This is the same for sexual harassment. It can be mitigated if the company implements the best security possible, which is creating an environment that is not conducive to sexual harassment.

Take a moment to compare the qualities:

Conducive	**Not Conducive**
Allows sexist or gender-based	Does not tolerate sexist or gender- jokes
Does not have a strong anti-harassment policy	Has a strong anti-harassment policy
Practices retaliation against	Investigates reports and does not

reporters of harassment   *retaliate against reporters of harassment*

All of the above responses cost companies tremendously. NEGATIVE BEHAVIORS AND TREATMENT OF VALUABLE EMPLOYEES CAN DAMAGE THE BOTTOM LINE.

Risk Factors for Sexual Harassment:

1. *Diverse culture with communication boundaries*
2. *Homogenous environment with mostly members of one gender*
3. *Many young employees*
4. *Language barriers between co-workers*
5. *A few "High Value" Employees*
6. *Significant hierarchical differences/rankings*
7. *Reliance on customer satisfaction*
8. *Slow or monotonous work environment*
9. *Decentralized work areas (separation)*
10. *Alcohol tolerance*

Is your company at risk?

If so, take the following steps to reduce that risk and avoid sexual harassment claims, complaints, and fault.

How To PROPERLY Avoid Sexual Harassment & Fault in the Workplace

After studying and practicing sexual harassment prevention, I have developed a strong and simple method for preventing workplace complaints and fault. Here are a few steps to take now:

1. **Evaluate Your Policy:** Does it clearly define behaviors that are considered sexual harassment? Does it clearly explain what should be done if these behaviors occur or are witnessed? Does it clearly explain what should be expected if sexual harassment is reported?

2. **Evaluate Your Training:** Do you have LIVE on-site training that allows for questions and answers? Do you have training that is memorable? Do you have training that addresses realistic scenarios based on your company? Do you have ongoing training?

3. **Implement Necessary Changes.**

4. **Evaluate Changes.**

5. **Enforce Policy Guidelines.**

In the wake of #MeToo and #TimesUp, many people have become fearful of this problem to the extent that they do not handle it. This is a vital mistake.

♦♦♦ Becoming Ideal ♦♦♦

My latest sexual harassment prevention training that I conducted took place in an ideal work environment. It is a nonprofit organization that helps inmates transition back into society so that they do not revisit the behaviors that landed them in trouble. The Executive Director expressed her concerns that after an incident happened between two co-workers that the organization's understanding of sexual harassment may need to be updated. She wanted to be pro-active rather than reactive, and she wanted her employees to recognize the serious approach that she was taking by calling in an expert.

I began my process by examining their policy, which was missing a few key ingredients. This is one of the first pieces of evidence in a sexual harassment claim against a company. If the policy is not clear, then the company can be in trouble for not providing the correct and complete information. It is actually very similar to a HAZARDOUS MATERIALS guide. If you are not thorough, and an incident happens, you are liable. However, these were easy fixes, and a simple email suffices to update the employees.

The next step in the process was to get to know the organization better so that I could customize the training. The director took me on a tour of the facilities and introduced me to some of the employees. Everyone seemed happy and comfortable in their respective environments. I felt as if this was a tight-knit family rather than a workplace. I developed my training with this in mind. Basically, I wanted to approach the training from the angle of giving people the benefit of a doubt and focus on communication.

The training went splendidly. All the attendees asked questions and gave feedback. This is one area where on-site, live training differs from online click-through slide training. There is an opportunity that exists where people can truly learn and understand that simply cannot be accomplished with slides and paragraphs and quizzes. Ultimately, this is because sexual harassment is never black and white. Most of the time, it does not happen in the same manner with the same circumstances. This is because it is a human problem, and humans have different experiences and personalities that feed their perceptions and actions.

...it [sexual harassment] is a human problem, and humans have different experiences and personalities that feed their perceptions and actions.

Returning to the example that Jody provides in relation to sexual harassment, her situation highlights this fact. Her situation was not that she was directly harassed by a superior, but she witnessed his inappropriate behavior on multiple occasions. She felt helpless because of her knowledge that he was related to their director and was not reprimanded for his behavior when it was reported. This put her in a position to be liable herself because she was responsible for her employees' safety and well-being. It also created a hostile work environment for her because she felt that the behavior reinforced negative treatment of women.

If we give Frank the benefit of the doubt and assume that he may not know that he is offending Jody, then how should this be handled? Frank needs coaching in sexual harassment prevention and understanding. He needs someone to be face-to-face with him and answer questions and present scenarios to him that may be unclear to him. He needs to understand that perception, not intention is the key in a sexual harassment situation. For instance, even if his intention is innocent, if the behavior is received as harassing or offensive, it can be considered sexual harassment under the law.

Taking this simple step would demonstrate to Jody that the organization sees the problem and is ready to remedy it. Doing nothing shows her that the company does not care. This is the attitude developed by companies who are protected by human resource providers and legal teams that are trained to protect the company, not the employees from sexual harassment. This is why the client that I mentioned was ideal. Although the nonprofit was protected by a human resource provider, the Executive Director saw that in order to create a better environment for her employees, she had to go beyond compliance.

Some other ways to prevent sexual harassment and improve the workplace culture include expressing respect, encouraging reporting, instituting proportional consequences, equipping bystanders, and promoting more women (Harvey & Fee, 2018).

To express respect, Harvey & Fee (2018) argue that companies should crowd out unwanted behaviors by emphasizing positive ones. They offer examples of ways to start off trainings by asking attendees to express respectful behavior with these questions: How do you treat someone with respect? How do you speak to others respectfully? What is an example of a positive exchange between co-workers?

Most sexual harassment goes unreported until it reaches a point that forces the recipient to report or leave out of desperation. If companies encourage reporting and make reporting a safe and easy process, this will be avoided.

Many people assume that the consequence for sexual harassment is firing, and this also leads to a lack of reporting. Recipients of sexual harassment do not necessarily want to get their co-worker fired. Instead, they usually just want the behavior to change so that they feel safe coming to work. Researchers suggest that a zero-tolerance policy is more hurtful than helpful (Harvey & Fee, 2018). Instead, consequences should be proportional to the offense (Harvey & Fee, 2018). Like the case with Frank, some actions merit education, while others may lead to separation or suspension. Only major offenses should result in firing.

Because recipients of sexual harassment are in such a vulnerable position, equipping bystanders can prevent a lot of negative behavior. Harvey & Fee (2018) reason that all employees should be taught to support one another and promote personal accountability in stopping sexual harassment. Part of this is emphasizing that saying or doing nothing is equivalent to enabling (Harvey & Fee, 2018). In training, all employees should be given the correct words to say to report all forms of harassment, direct and indirect.

Finally, research shows that companies with more women in management have less sexual harassment (Harvey & Fee, 2018). So, if companies really want to prevent harassment in their workplace, they will promote more women to management positions.

Hiding from sexual harassment and diversity issues under a compliance-based system is no longer a valid plan. Although a legal team or human resource management may provide a wall of protection for the company, these do not protect the people. Since these are people-related problems, companies who want to seek success will recognize them and take action to prevent them.

Mistake #5:
Curve 'n Foul

PITCHING A PROPOSAL THAT LEADS TO NOTHING

FOULS MAY NOT BE THE WORST HITS IN BASEBALL, BUT FOULING IN BUSINESS CAN LEAD TO MANY OUTS. One of the biggest fouls is to offer something in desperation rather than making actual changes. Assuming that problems can be solved with money demonstrates a lack of understanding of people and relationships. Money may serve as a band-aid, covering the wound for a while, but eventually the scars left by negative treatment will outweigh the temporary fix. People, especially the best and the brightest, have needs beyond financial advances, such as being fulfilled and treated with respect.

Throwing money at problems in business is like buying a house to fix a relationship, or worse, having a baby. Many people think that problems will go away if something is put in the way of them. However, many problems are deeply rooted and cannot be covered up. They must be dealt with directly and solved.

Jody provides yet another good example. When she first expressed her discontent, her director offered her more money. He was able to give her a significant raise. She took it and convinced herself that this would help to balance out the problems that she was having.

♦♦♦ The Foul ♦♦♦

A few weeks later, the discontentment returned, and the money was now a problem rather than a solution.

This is because money is a basic need that does not get close to the true needs of people. Many theories have demonstrated this. One of these is Maslow's Hierarchy of Needs, which is a motivational theory in psychology comprising a five-tier model of human needs, often depicted as hierarchical levels within a pyramid (McLeod, 2018). Money falls into the lowest two levels of the pyramid. It provides the basic needs of food and water, security and safety. However, once these needs are met, a person is motivated to move up the triangle to psychological and self-fulfillment needs.

In the example with Jody, she had already met her basic needs. She was making a sufficient income to meet her basic needs and even go above them for luxury. However, the problems that she was facing at work were negatively impacting her esteem needs and her self-actualization needs. She felt that she was not living up to her full potential because of the demands of her job.

Hierarchical Needs

People's needs for money are low on Maslow's Hierarchy of Needs:

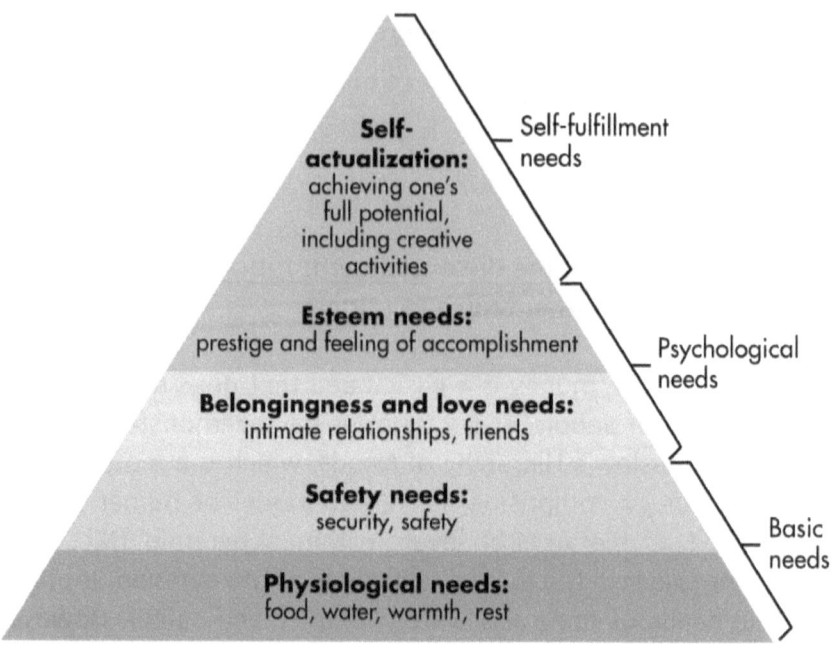

Not understanding people and their needs can lead to major failures in recruiting and retaining the best and the brightest employees. ONCE PEOPLE HAVE HAD THEIR BASIC NEEDS MET, THEY ARE ONLY MOTIVATED BY SELF-FULFILLMENT AND SELF-ACTUALIZATION NEEDS. THIS MEANS THAT COMPANIES MUST HELP THEM REACH THEIR FULL POTENTIAL RATHER THAN GETTING IN THE WAY OF IT.

Is Your Company Preventing People from Achieving Self-Actualization and Fulfillment?

1. *Are employees bogged down with pettty and mindless tasks when they could be demonstrating and utilizing their talents elsewhere?*
2. *Are leaders expected to deal with daily senseless complaints brought on by a lack of consequences for such complaints?*
3. *Are employees discouraged from seeking education or personal development opportunities in lieu of "duties" and "responsibilities"?*
4. *Are creative employees discouraged from employing their talents because they do not necessarily align with "company procedures"?*
5. *Are problems preventing employees from being fulfilled and growing to their fullest potential?*

Are you causing fouls?

If so, consider taking these measures to help employees be more likely to reach self-fulfillment in their careers:

How To Assist Employees in Reaching Fulfillment and Job Satisfaction

1. IDENTIFY STRENGTHS: Test employees and determine where they excel.
2. ASSIGN STRENGTH-BASED DUTIES.
3. ENCOURAGE EDUCATION.
4. ENCOURAGE CREATIVE THINKING.
5. INVEST IN EMPLOYEE EDUCATION AND ADVANCEMENT.
6. CREATE INCENTIVE PROGRAMS THAT ENCOURAGE GROWTH AND DEVELOPMENT.
7. PROVIDE OPPORTUNITIES FOR EMPLOYEES TO GIVE BACK (CHARITABLE EVENTS, COMMUNITY SUPPORT, ETC.).
8. ENCOURAGE EMPLOYEES TO BE INVOLVED IN GIVING BACK.

Many of these suggestions return to previous chapters. Basically, all of this goes back to building a better culture and organizational environment, but this chapter calls for you to do so with the employees' fulfillment in mind.

Recognizing employees' strengths and assigning duties based on them can help an employee grow, but encouraging them to take on challenging duties can also do the same.

Part of fulfillment is continued growth and development through education. This does not necessarily refer to traditional education courses but can involve continuing education courses. For instance, perhaps an employee has always been interested in art but has not had time to take classes. Provide a flexible schedule that allows the employee to take an art class. If your budget permits, you may also develop a program that covers some or all of the costs of attending continued education courses. Although this may seem like an endeavor that will not benefit the company, it will show employees that they are valued, and it will help them feel like they are moving up the hierarchical pyramid towards fulfillment.

Another part of fulfillment is being able to practice altruism or giving back. Many great companies provide opportunities for their employees to give back to their communities in some way. This not only helps employees feel fulfilled, but it also adds to the company's corporate social responsibility, which will not go unnoticed.

♦♦♦ Reaching Fulfillment ♦♦♦

Just like people need to be fulfilled, so do companies. A company that goes beyond the basic needs of meeting financial goals will also reap the benefits.

Providing employees with means to reaching higher self-awareness and self-fulfillment will provide the employer with more loyal employees. Business people do not have to be told what this means. You know that loyal and happy employees will be more productive and will be more likely to make customers happy and loyal too.

Building a community-based philanthropy program will also help the company tremendously. This is not difficult to do as there are many organizations that need simple tasks. For example, the company could become involved in a local food-bank, and they usually only need volunteers during certain times. Or, the company could take donations for holidays or disasters. The task does not have to be a major one, but it should be meaningful. To be successful, ask employees what they would be interested in doing for the project.

> ...This is not difficult...The task does not have to be a major one, but it should be meaningful.

This chapter began discussing the fact that Jody was unhappy, so her director tried to give her more money to appease her, which was a temporary fix. Examining the cause of this problem reveals that it goes back to the hierarchy of needs. Humans need much more than money. Money may help them get some of their needs met, but in the long run, money is not enough. After all, the old adage, "The more you make the more you spend," is true, and studies have even shown that most people who have more money are less happy than those who have less.

This reminds me of one of the first teachings of Buddhism: everyone suffers. Even those with money suffer. The key is to recognize why we are suffering, and that goes back to not having the need for self-actualization and fulfillment met.

Chapter 6:

Review Workbook

*GETTING THE WIN BY
BUILDING THE RIGHT TEAM
THE RIGHT WAY*

NOTHING FEELS BETTER THAN GETTING THE WIN. If a workplace is full of unhappy employees, nobody wins. And, that feeling of losing happens daily. This can lead to burnout and quite frankly, depression. This is why we must constantly work to improve ourselves as leaders and our environments for those that we are leading. This starts with recognizing our mistakes and making positive changes to avoid making them again. This book has presented only five mistakes observed, but they are a good start to making lasting changes and improvements to the workplace culture and organizational environment.

Use this last section to review the concepts and steps for making those positive changes. Applying the concepts discussed, develop the following plans.

Becoming the BATNA

Vision Statement: Write it out.

Value-Based Actions: What are some actions that you can take to illustrate the values addressed in the Vision?

Evaluation Process/Plan: How will you evaluate the BATNA?

Team Building Candidacy Project

Plan: What is the plan for a team building candidacy project?

Timeframe/Budget: What is the timeframe and budget for the project?

Launch: How will the launch be implemented?

Evaluation Process: How will you evaluate the project?

Poison Control

Problem(s): Try to determine any evident and existing problems.

Survey Questions: Develop survey questions for an opportunity for employees to report problems anonymously.

Investigation Plan: What are the methods that will be used to investigate the problems reported?

Action Plan: What is the plan to eliminate the problems identified?

Preventing Sexual Harassment

Policy: Does the current policy address the procedure for reporting, the expectations for the process, and the consequences of misconduct?

Training Plan: Does the training plan include bringing in an expert to do on-site training? Is it ongoing?

Enforcement: Do all employees and members of management understand that misconduct will not be tolerated?

Evaluation Process/Plan: How will you evaluate the process?

Growth and Development

Method for Identifying Strengths: How will you find employees' strengths?

Strength-Based Assignments: What assignments can you give based on the strengths identified?

Education and Creative Thinking Implementation Plan: Develop a plan for implementing education and creative thinking.

Evaluation Plan: How will you evaluate the projects?

REFERENCES

Fisher, R. & Ury, W. (2011). *Getting to Yes: Negotiating Agreement without Giving In.* Penguin: NY.

Harvey, E. & Fee, S. (2018). *Stop Workplace Sexual Harassment, Quickly & Permanently.* Walk the Talk: TX.

Walker, J. (2013). *Introduction to Hospitality Management.* 4th Ed. Pearson: Boston.

About the Author

Julie Still-Rolin is a Pensacola, Florida based creative entrepreneur. She is the founder of two companies: Still-Rolin Associates, a business consulting firm, and Evolve 'n Thrive, an event hosting company. Years of teaching and developing curriculum combined with her family's background in small business led her to develop solutions for companies.

Her first book, *The End Game: A Training Guide for Those Who Truly Want to End Sexual Harassment* provides research into the motivations of respondents pertaining to personality traits. She used this research and more to direct her simple yet effective sexual harassment prevention training for organizations.

Julie is also a national speaker on various topics including diversity, sexuality, personal growth and development. Some of these stemmed from her second book, *Evolving through Bullshit: Getting to a Better Place Despite Obstacles*.

Julie is the proud mother of two beautiful and challenging young people. Her wife, Alisa, is often the inspiration and support for her writing. Her family enjoys the beach and spending quiet time together when they're not traveling for work or leisure.

About Still-Rolin Associates. LLC

Still-Rolin Associates, LLC provides both professional and personal development services, including:

➤ Writing courses geared for self-publishing or combination of traditional and self-publishing

➤ Writing Coaching to help people get to the finish line with their book along with marketing and other assistance

➤ Access to speakers for engagement

➤ Professional development courses

➤ Sexual harassment prevention training

To learn more, visit www.juliestillrolin.com

www.ingramcontent.com/pod-product-compliance
Lightning Source LLC
Chambersburg PA
CBHW030735180526
45157CB00008BA/3176